# EXISTENCE OF
# GOD

# EXISTENCE OF
# GOD

## S C SAWHNEY

PARTRIDGE

A Penguin Random House Company

**To order additional copies of this book, contact**
Partridge India
000 800 10062 62
orders.india@partridgepublishing.com

www.partridgepublishing.com/india

# Contents

## <u>What Is New in the Book? - A Synopsis</u>

1.  The book stipulates that Baba Vanga may have visioned the illuminated rooms of the hotels being planned to be built in the space only as the New Star System in her prophesy that predicts that man may move out to a New Star System in the year 3797.

2.  It comes out in support of the belief of Hindus that Rama was born in Treta Yuga while Krishna was born in Dwapar Yuga and that Kali Yuga started with the end of Mahabharata by spelling out exact spans of various Yugas on the basis of 3000 years per Yuga overlapping them over "Stone Age".

3.  It stipulates that the millions of floating stones that must have gone into the construction of Ram Setu may have been sourced from either Kumari Kandam or the U-Shaped Structure believed to have existed at the time of the construction of the bridge according to CSIR - National Institute of Oceanography but may have been swallowed by the sea over a span of time.

4.  It argues why Ram Setu should not be considered to be a tombolo as listed under Wikipedia.

5.  It says kudos to the natural Water Recycling System of the Earth which not only purifies the water, recharges the subterranean water and redistributes the water making it available all over the Earth also ensures that not even a single drop of water gets lost in the process.

6.  It introduces the phrase of being ON LINE with the God.

7.  It draws attention toward the fact that hardly 0.1 % of the Sun Rays emitted by the Sun fall on the planets, the satellites of the planets and the asteroids, the remaining 99.9 % rays keep on traveling deep into space wondering whether these get scavenged for reuse or not. If these rays simply get lost should it not be considered as a lapse on the part of the so called Supreme God of whom we so firmly think, could have not allowed an outright wastage of such a magnitude of not only solar energy but even any other form of energy?

8.  It asserts, "If we don't doubt that Shakuntala Devi's brain had the capability of working just like a supercomputer why should we be so reluctant to submit to the possibility of Natalya Demkina's brain doubling up like an X-Ray machine?"

# Preface

At the outset the author tells that God may not come down from the heavens to convince us whether He exists or not. So we have to find out the truth about Him ourselves only.

Next, he focuses our attention on the fact that a time has arrived when we should think afresh about the existence of God based on the present level of our intellect since the intellect of the people who had originally evolved the concepts of God was very poor for many understandable reasons as compared to the present level of our intellect which seems to have reached almost a pinnacle.

He hints at their extremely low intellect by pointing at the following aspects.

(i) Galileo Galilei had to bear extreme humiliation during his life just to have made them aware that earth revolves around the sun not the sun around the earth as they used to believe and it had taken them as long as 359 years to have changed their misconception.

(ii) They had a notion that the sun and the moon disappear during solar and lunar eclipses because some demon must be devouring them while today even a school-going child knows that the sun and the moon disappear only when either the moon hides the view of sun or the shadow of earth falls on the moon.

(iii) They had a notion that earth must be shaking during the earth quakes when the God may be getting angry with them not because of slippage of the lower layers of earth under the upper layers of earth as is well known to all of us.

The author tries to explain the reasons of the science being so averse to the concepts of God by explaining on one side why anyone who should have created the Universe ought to have been neither animate nor inanimate at the time of creation of the Universe and on the other side highlighting that anything that may be neither animate nor inanimate does not find access to the portals of the science. Besides it what disables the scientists to find the truth about God lies in some1 of their self-imposed restraints only.

For instance, though they ascertained the value of Gravitational Constant it did not occur to any of them that they should have also thought who could have settled for this particular value of the Constant. Or would whosoever may have decided its value have also explored what impact a value other than $6.674 \times 10^{-11}$ N·m$^2$/kg$^2$, could have had on the constitution of the Universe that had yet to come up into existence?

This figure must have not been picked up by Him just out of hat. He must have also found out why its value should have been $6.674 \times 10^{-11}$ N·m$^2$/kg$^2$ only not some other value, say, $5.674 \times 10^{-11}$ N·m$^2$/kg$^2$ or $7.674 \times 10^{-11}$ N·m$^2$/kg$^2$ quite ahead of the creation of the Universe. Is it difficult to guess, whosoever would have taken such decision couldn't have been some human being? Question arises, if not a human being who should have closed down the bet? Or do you think everything should have gone about in an unplanned manner only?

He has stressed that we should believe in the existence of God mainly because every system such as the recycling of water bears a stamp of so high a level of intelligence that no human beings could be perceived to have had when such systems should have been evolved instead of any other reason and should pay Him regard for having made us so intelligent as we are and so capable of exercising our own discretion as we are able to exercise more than for any other reasons since whatever we are today, we are because of our intelligence and our power of exercising own discretions only more than anything else.

To delineate the material picked up from other sources such as Internet, such material has been italicised in the book for demarcation.

# 1

## The Origin of the Concept of God

The way various constellations, the bright sun, the silvery moon and so many stars we see in the sky should have come up may be controversial but it is not difficult to trace the history of the evolution of the concept of God.

Not being able to make out who may have created the Universe the primeval men and women must have thought, God only should have created everything they could see around them.

They may have been taken by awe when they must have seen lava being erupted by the volcanoes because they did not know volcanoes are caused when the magna beneath the Earth's crust finds a pathway to the surface. They may have got frightened when they must have seen the earth getting jolted by the earthquakes because they did not know that the earthquakes occur when the lower layers of earth slip beneath the upper layers of the earth or by seeing the sun and the moon disappearing during the eclipses because they did not know that eclipses occur when either the shadow of the earth falls on moon or the moon hides the view of sun or the rivers getting flooded.

They may have thought that such events occur when the God may be angry with them. So they started worshipping the God by performing *pujas*[1] to please Him.

Many of them may have thought that the stars twinkling in the sky could have been the Gods who keep on watching us. So whenever they may have been in some trouble they may have started looking up toward the sky to seek their blessings.

At the same time the frightening scenes of the dreams and the gruelling scenes of deaths must have led them to develop the concepts of souls and ghosts over a time.

In between they should have also developed the concepts of heaven (or paradise) and hell and ultimately may have started giving their beliefs the shape of religions.

They may have been quite wise but they certainly did not know whether sun rotates around the earth or the other way round, the earth around the sun. Though today everybody knows that earth rotates around the sun they believed that sun should have been rotating around the earth.

Over millennia of years they must have evolved several religions based on their beliefs. But their beliefs got so well entrenched in their minds that when Galileo Galilei told them that the earth moved around the sun, not the other way round as they thought, way back in 1610 based on the observations made by him through the telescope built by him to observe the solar system the clerics started ridiculing him because it contradicted the Bible. So the Church declared Galileo Galilei to be a heretic and did not take any time to persecute him for having had the guts of contradicting the Bible.

His observation triggered a debate for as long as 359 years since it was not till 31 October 1991 when Pope John Paul II publically acknowledged that the Church had erred in condemning Galileo.

As a matter of fact even back in 1600, a man named Giordano Bruno had been even burnt to death for believing that the earth moved around the sun and there were many planets throughout the universe where life should have existed.

How much people are afraid of religious extremists can be easily gauged from the fact that the person who has posted the drafts of his phenomenal book tentatively titled as "Love Letters of Grampa -- about Life, Liberty and the Zen of Zero" on his website zenofzero.net in response to the query "Grampa, how come you don't believe in God?" of his four year granddaughter, has not disclosed his identity to protect his grandchildren from retaliation by them or may be even himself keeping in mind the oppressive journey of Galileo Galilei.

In the draft "/docs/1x09 ChangingGods.pdf" he has pointed out that people developed very strange and hazy ideas about Gods because of astoundingly slow development of the intellect between 6600 and 2200 BCE. He has drawn an analogy between the level of the "awareness" of the people during various astrological ages and the "awareness" of the modern people at the different ages of their lives during various astrological ages, as shown by him in the following table[2].

| Time Period | Astrological Age | Awareness Level |
|---|---|---|
| Before ~ 6600 BCE | Before the Age of Gemini | Infants |
| ~ 6600 - ~ 4400 BCE | Gemini (the twin) | Preschoolers |
| ~ 4400 - ~ 2200 BCE | Taurus (the bull) | Preteens |
| ~ 2200 - ~ 0 BCE | Aires (the lamb) | Teenagers |
| ~ 0 CE - ~ 2200 CE | Pisces (the fish) | Young Adults |
| ~ 2200 - ~ 4400 CE | Aquarius (the water carrier) | Adults |

He has given above projections to impress what people could have pictured in the eclipses, volcanoes or earth quakes and floods with such "awareness levels" between about 6600 and 4400 BCE or prior to that. The Romans and the Hindus besides the Greeks, in particular, went ahead with the idea of picturing several Gods and Goddesses, like the God of death, the God of love, The God of rains and the God of wind in their scriptures.

But the clerics do not seem to have reacted the same way at the assertion, "God did not create the Universe and the 'Big Bang' was an inevitable consequence of the laws of physics.

The fact that there is a law such as gravity, the Universe can and will create itself from nothing." made by Stephen Hawking the legendary theoretical physicist and Leonard Mlodinow in their book "The Grand Design", published in year 2012 even though the concept they talk about, which they have named as 'M-theory', makes 'Creator of the Universe' redundant.

God may or may have not created the Universe all right but God ought to have played a big role in the evolution of the fauna and flora.

The concept of God having created all species of the fauna seems to have stemmed from the age-old dilemma whether dinosaurs should have had come into existence first or their eggs. If eggs would have come first who could have brought them and from where they could have been brought? Only dinosaurs could have laid them. But dinosaurs could have not come from anywhere had there been no eggs. Struck up in a loop, the only plausible way of getting out of the loop was to believe that God ought to have created not only the dinosaurs but even all other species of the fauna and flora, first.

However such a belief must have led them yet to one more equally puzzling riddle, "If God created all types of fauna and flora who ought to have created the God?"

The only way of getting out of this quandary that may have appeared to be most plausible to them could have been to believe that God could not have had a predecessor. So He ought to have been a Self-born Entity, *"Swayambhoo"* as He is widely acclaimed to be by the Hindus.

Though the concept of God may have been apparently a product of our ancestors' mind only, we can't deny that we feel comforted by the thoughts of God when we are in trouble.

It is also true that if we have faith in Him, we feel less encumbered in our life.

Over a time, people also started thinking that God being so powerful, could probably come to their rescue when they may be in trouble and may not see any succour coming from any corner.

But a question that rakes our mind constantly is, "What would have happened if we did not have the 'intelligence to understand things' or 'the power of exercising our own discretion'?"

We are what we are today merely due to our intelligence only.

Undeniably both of these attributes are our most valuable attributes. So naturally we also thought, who should have imparted us these attributes? Though we may not know who may have been so benevolent to us as to have made us so intelligent we should not hesitate to admit that we regard the One who may have given us these attributes only as "God".

As a matter of fact everything seems to have been so intelligently planned out for our planet that we can't assume that even moon would have become a satellite of earth just by chance. Surely it ought to have been also planned out to have been there. So we may believe that He only should have conceived that if the earth had a moon it would be able to light up the earth through moonlight even during the nights. Today we are able to light the whole city by electric light but we invented electricity pretty late. It is only He who may have provided to us light through moon during the nights till we did not invent electricity or lamps.

And do you know how the moon of Earth came into existence? It is believed that a meteor dislodged a chunk of Earth when it had hit the Earth. Certainly it could have not been just a matter of chance that some meteor should have hit the Earth. Since God realized that it was necessary that Earth had a moon so that it did not remain dark during the nights it is quite possible that He only must have used the meteor to make the earth safe as well as more picturesque.

How much we owe to Him for having taken such a step to create the moon?

We also owe to Him for having created a foolproof automatic system of purification of water by recycling the water by combining the process of evaporation and the process of condensation to convert it into clouds to fall back on the earth in the form of rains to recharge the subterranean water as well as let them traverse the sky to get deposited as snow on the mountains to melt and flow back toward seas through rivers, round the year since very beginning while we could develop the technique of purifying water by exposing it to ultraviolet rays only after the discovery of the ultraviolet rays.

If we stretch our imagination a bit it would not be difficult to find out many other things for which we could heap lots of accolades on Him.

What would have happened if ultraviolet rays would have not been there? Would we still have been able to purify water by exposing it to ultraviolet rays?

So many things could have not occurred by themselves since all of them bear a stamp of extraordinary intelligence. So there should have been somebody possessing extraordinary intelligence that should have developed all such systems. Whether we know Him or not does not matter, but we should at least not disgrace Him by saying, "We don't know whether He exists or not?"

Actually nothing can be more outrageous and more discourteous on our part than to do not acknowledge His existence.

We have to believe in His existence mainly because of immense intelligence that has apparently gone into everything.

He would surely not descend from the heavens to convince us whether He exists or not. He had not descended to tell us even about the atomic structures and many other things we did not know earlier. It depends on us whether we find Him or not. So why should we expect that He should descend to prove His existence? It is for us to find out His hiding and make up our mind whether to respect Him or not.

---

1 Hindi word for the processes of worshipping the God
2 Reproduced from www.zenofzero.net with permission of A Zoroaster, the owner of the website

# 2

## God and Soul, Parmatma and Atma in Hinduism

We cannot access anybody who may have witnessed creation of Universe. Even if we knew who may have witnessed the process of evolution there is no chance we could ever locate him. Actually he could have not been somebody who could "think". The Universe ought to have got evolved in a natural course. Even if we could have located him we may not be able to understand the language in which he may converse with us. As a matter of fact no language may have been even evolved when the process of evolution may have taken place.

We don't even know how such big animals as dinosaurs could have come into existence. We are not in a position to ascertain even their antecedents. All we know about them is, they may have died due to some natural calamity or got burnt by some meteors that may have struck the earth long back and got dumped several crusts of earth down below the ground to have been converted into petroleum. We also do not know whether we are diminutives of the same dinosaurs or are a form of an altogether different species. Since no written documents had been prepared when they disappeared we may only try to speculate how they may have died or how Homo sapiens may have evolved based on anthropological studies only.

If we are not able to explore even much about the dinosaurs that existed on the earth during the Mesozoic Era about 230 million years ago do you think we can guess much about the origin of the Universe which is believed to have come into existence billions of years back or ever-existent God, who is believed to have created the Universe?

But think of the evolution of the Homo sapiens on the planets from where they may have arrived on the earth. Somebody must have evolved them even on those planets. It prompts us to think, who could have been that "somebody" who should have been able to create them on those planets? It has to be the same someone whom we call "God", one who is believed to be *"Anadi"* according to Hindus, implying thereby that He has been in existence ever since and would continue to live forever.

We may perhaps find some connection through our souls which are considered to be eternal since the God is also said to be eternal. But how much do we know even about the souls? All we know about the souls is that they are vital for us since they part us when we die and we die when they part us. All we know is when we are reborn, some soul joins us again. But we still don't know where the souls reside. We cannot acquire a soul of our choice either. With regard to the soul we may be allotted we are totally helpless. We have to acquire the soul that may be allotted to us.

We have not been able to find out how the souls get allotted nor perhaps may we ever decode this secret.

With such a poor knowledge about the souls how may we ever expect to know anything about the God?

As we know everything has to be either animate or inanimate. But God is hopefully neither animate nor inanimate. So high must have been the temperature of the dark energy or dark matter (or Baryonic matter) that ought to have burst into Big Bangs that no animate object could have existed anywhere around the Big Bangs. Nor any inanimate object could have had the level of intelligence supervision of such big events as Big Bangs should have called for. So whosoever may have monitored the Big Bangs could have been neither an animate object nor an inanimate object. This is perhaps the reason why we premise that God is neither animate nor inanimate.

If He is neither animate nor inanimate, a question arises what He possibly is?

We find an answer to this question in the article "God and Soul, Atma and Paramatma, in Hinduism" of V Jayaraman published by "Hinduwebsite.com".

In this article he says, according to Hindus it is not possible for anyone to know for sure the true equation between God and His creation in a wakeful state nor are we able to say conclusively whether they are the same or different.

Though philosophers and scholars have been exploring and speculating about it since the ancient times, but as history proves they have not been able to reach a conclusion.

He equates God and the Supreme Self and says since both the Self and the Supreme Self are beyond the mind and body; neither of them can be grasped with the senses or the intellect. Hence nothing can be proved about them empirically or in a wakeful state, except through an inner personal spiritual experience.

According to Hinduism there is no distinction of duality between God and the soul except in our perception. God and the soul are one and the same.

It is a concept that cannot be clarified or explained by anyone to our complete satisfaction. One has to arrive at the truth by himself and experience the transcendental state personally.

In another article "The Concept of Atman or Eternal Self in Hinduism" he says, Atman, the Self that is, the soul is the immortal aspect of the mortal existence and lf, which is hidden in every object of creation including man and tells that according to Hindus, "*The Self is the silent partner in all our deeds and experiences, the observer and the indweller of all embodied beings. Its nature cannot be explained or described in human language adequately, as it is beyond the senses and mind. There the eyes cannot travel, nor speech nor mind.*"

But Hindus premise that we can certainly communicate with Him through our souls.

As we know the concepts of God had been evolved when nobody knew even whether earth revolves around the sun or the earth around the sun. It was when people thought some demon may be devouring the sun during the solar eclipse and the moon during the lunar eclipse while today even a school going child knows that the sun and the moon appear to disappear during eclipses only when either moon hides the view of sun or the shadow of earth falls on the moon.

So it is high time we looked at the concepts of God afresh with the present level of our intellect.

For instance we have to agree that He ought to have known everything about the molecular structures for having created so many elements and so many salts in the world. He must have known everything about nuclear fusion for having created so many suns. He ought to have known everything about the gravitational forces and the centrifugal forces for having evolved the self- balancing system of the planets and the satellites of the planets. He ought to have known everything about the stem cells and biology for having created such a vast variety of fauna in the world. He ought to have also known everything about botany for having created such a variety of flora in the world. Can we believe that anyone may have known everything about so many things without having ever gone to any school? But He ought to have known not only what we know today but even what we still do not know.

Though we may be happy that we have ascertained the value of the Gravitational Constant, if we want to get satisfied that God only should have decided its value we have to think who, if not God, could have decided that it should have been $6.674 \times 10^{-11}$ N·m²/kg² only, not $5.674 \times 10^{-11}$ N·m²/kg² or $7.674 \times 10^{-11}$ N·m²/kg²?

We should also think that somebody must have definitely deliberated over this issue.

We should also think, who could have thought of the criteria based on which a decision should have been taken on the most appropriate value of the Gravitational Co nstant. Surely someone must have gone into all the related aspects before arriving at this value. Whom do you think would have deliberated over this issue? Obviously no human beings, by any chance!

The moment we come to the conclusion that it could have not been a human being we have no other option than to believe that it could have been only God, none else.

# 3

## GPS of the Brains

The husband and wife team, May-Britt Moser and Edvard I. Moser who work at the Norwegian University of Science and Technology in Trondheim shared the Nobel Prize for discovering the brain's "GPS system" in 2014 with the UK-based researcher Prof John O'Keefe. Mosers had discovered in 2005 the part of the brain which has "grid cells" that are akin to lines of longitude and latitude, helping the brain to judge distance and navigate which act more like a nautical chart. But I have some other reason to feel happy that they could have discovered how the brain knows where we are and lets us navigate from one place to another through our subconscious mind.

This discovery answers the query that had been puzzling me since 1961 when my younger brother Dr Satish had come to meet me at Delhi when I used to live at the humble Railway Colony of Sewa Nagar. My brother was only 13 years old at that time and had come to Delhi for the first time. Since he came exactly during the International Trade Fare days I took him to the Trade Fare. We went on foot from our house all the way along with some of our neighbours.

When we were roaming around in the Fare I got struck up at a book stall a little too long. Though my brother prodded me to leave the stall and move to other stalls and pavilions but I did not listen to him. So he moved on to watch other stalls of the Fare alone. When I turned around after a short while, I could not keep myself composed. I searched for him everywhere but could not locate him anywhere. So I went to the public announcement booth and got the message announced that he should come to meet me at the booth. But he did not turn up at the booth. I felt very uneasy because I did not know how I was going to explain to my parents that he had gone missing at the Fare. After seeing me to have waited for as long as two to three hours, the manager opined that had he been anywhere around he would have surely turned up at the booth. So he advised that he could have as well gone back. So I should better go back instead of waiting there. So despondingly I left the ground to return to my tenement.

Since I had not given him any money I was worried that he couldn't have hired an auto rickshaw or purchased a ticket to travel by bus. Even if he may have had some money he couldn't have hired the auto rickshaw or travelled by bus as he had never been to any big city like Delhi earlier. But when I reached home I got stunned to find that he could have gone back all the way on foot without any difficulty. Nor did he have to ask anyone on the way about the route.

That was the first time I realized that our brains may be also having a GPS of the type we nowadays have in our cars that helps us through the routes we may follow when we want to go somewhere.

This discovery incidentally also answers the puzzle how the honey bees may be managing to trace back their route to their own honeycombs after collecting the nectar of flowers from places far away from their honeycombs even when many other honeycombs may be also hanging on the same tree. Though it is not known yet, may be they too have a GPS at their disposal.

All systems developed by the Nature seem to be need-based. Nature may have evolved the GPS for us since so many people especially the children so often get lost in the Fares. The same may have been the case with honeybees also. Our mind may be keeping the track of our needs to help us in the process.

Since my brother did not face any difficulty in coming back from the Fare I think we are not only able to look back into our past events as if we are viewing the past life through a rear view mirror our brain starts recording whatever we may see through this mirror in the form of a road map in our subconscious memory whenever we visit a new place.

Not being sure of such a system many people have the tendency of noting down the route or committing the route to memory so that they do not miss the route afterwards. Even those of us who maybe knowing that we have such a system may not like to take a chance outright until we ascertain whether we may depend on it or not. But surely such GPS should help us if we do not make any conscious effort to remember the new routes we may use.

Don't you think it is quite startling that we have a GPS in our brain? Whom do we owe for it? Who else but the God? But to thank Him, we have to first believe that He exists. Isn't?

# 4

# Waste Control Systems of God

Surely when God must have created the Universe He must have evolved suitable waste control systems also.

For a break, let us think about the recycling system of water that ensures complete recirculation of water on the earth without any wastage. Don't you think every drop of water gets recycled? Not a single drop of water seems to get lost in the process. First of all, it gets converted into vapour. The vapour gets converted into clouds next. Some clouds go right up to the mountains to get deposited there in the form of snow and some of them burst into rains. The clouds fall back on the earth in the form of water again which flows back to the oceans or other water bodies. Some of the water gets absorbed by the earth to become subterranean water. But every drop of water gets recycled. Nothing escapes the earth except what we may send out into space through rockets.

So there is a reason to believe that He must have evolved suitable system for the recycling of all forms of energies including the solar energy as well without letting it squatter or get squandered.

As we know matter may get converted into energy and the energy converted back into matter according to the Einstein's formula $E = m . C^2$. But perhaps nothing gets permanently annihilated in the Universe. Though looking at the mass of all the planets and all other celestial bodies of the Universe we get dumbfounded to think of the quantity of energy that should have gone into their evolution according to Einstein's formula, it is unlikely that He would have not worked on the principle of "Zero Wastage" of the solar energy by ensuring recycling of the solar rays of light that do not fall on any of the planets, any of the asteroids or any of the satellites of the planets.

Since the sun and the space in which all the planets revolve around it looks like a doughnut, obviously only a minuscule of the solar rays must be falling on the planets or the asteroids and the satellites of the planets. Think of the enormous energy that must be escaping into the space through the semi-spheres above and below this spatial disc. Think further, should all these rays of light be travelling unto eternity to get finally lost somewhere or such rays must be also getting recycled?

As of now, we have no idea whether the rays of light that don't fall on any planets or asteroids and satellites simply keep on travelling farther deep into space unto eternity or get "recycled".

Surely He would have been neither so lavish nor so reckless as to have let so much solar energy get lost. He must have evolved some system of trapping it somehow.

Not even 0.1 % of sun rays emitted by the suns may be falling on the planets or asteroids and satellites. How vast is the space above and beneath the spatial disc in which the planets revolve, the remaining 99.9 % solar rays must be passing through? What may be happening to the major part of the rays that escape the spatial discs?

God could have not been so lavish as to have utilized only about 0.1 % of the energy generated by the suns and have let the remaining energy get squandered.

Don't you think He must have developed some system of recycling the lion's share of the solar rays shown in the following diagram that do not get intercepted by the planets or the asteroids and the satellites of the suns?

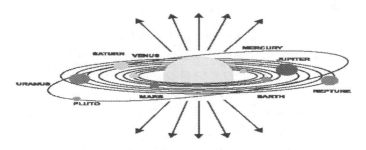

*Solar Rays that Do not Fall on the Planets,*
*the Satellites or the Asteroids*

We have a reason to believe the way He We have a reason to believe the way He had evolved a system that did not allow did not allow wastage of even a single drop of water surely He would have evolved an equally efficient system to avoid any wastage of the precious solar energy emitted by the suns also.

Don't you think, not making any use of so much energy can be thought of being only a big lapse on His part?

If we have not been able to find even a slight lapse or slightest flaw in any of other systems evolved by Him, we have no reason to suspect that He would have slurred in case of solar energy. He has shown a superb level of perfection in all the systems. He is actually a synonym of perfection. So why would He have not tried to trap the energy that escapes the thin slice of space in which the planets revolve?

We have to only find how the entire energy being emitted by the suns since their evolution must be getting utilized without any wastage. He should have not prepared His mind to do not feel concerned about so much of energy that the suns would be emitting till they get old and stop functioning, getting squandered.

If it may not be getting recycled He must have found some way of utilizing it for sure.

We may pin our hopes only on a Space Agency of the rank of NASA or some other Space Agency worth the salt to come out with an answer.

But for sure, if NASA or some other agency finds out whether some system of recycling of the escaping solar energy exists or not or how this energy probably gets utilized, it would be a landmark of a sort that would bring us one more step closer to the God.

Do we know the source of the energy that gets sucked into the black holes? It is quite possible that the bulk of the solar energy that escapes deep into space may be getting sucked into the black holes because God may have not reconciled to such a colossal loss of solar energy. If not this energy, which other energy may be getting sucked into the black holes? Surely God could have not been so careless or so casual about the energy that keeps on escaping into space continuously.

# 5

# Life Is Simply a 'Hide and Seek' Game

The concept of destiny dawned on us due to the belief that sometimes we get struck up in a situation over which we could have probably not have had any control. For a while let us assume that such situations arise in our life due to our destiny. Whether we like or not, we have to essentially cross over to them.

Such situations are usually unpredictable.

Just think of a situation, we may have been planning to do something but it may start raining cats and dogs on that day or some other more urgent work may compel us to change our schedule. We believe that such situations arise in our life due to our destiny.

We usually vaguely relegate occurrence of such situations to our stars though we really don't know whether stars may or may not have any role in the game plan of our destiny.

Destiny can take someone sky high all too sudden. It may even kill our all ambitions without our getting any inkling.

Destiny is like the rear side of the moon which we are not able to see from the earth. Yet it does not imply that the moon may not be having a rear side at all. The same way we also have a destiny that hangs around us all the time.

But it is not easy to decode the destiny. We come to know about our destiny only when it opens its cards on the table.

For instance, take the example of Manjunath who had done his MBA from the IIM, Lucknow in the year 2003. Could he have ever known that he would be murdered by a mafia because he would not allow him to contaminate petrol at his petrol pump in Lakhimpur Kheri district? Had he known, perhaps he would have not committed such a mistake if we at all call it a mistake. Because he could not tolerate that somebody should adulterate petrol in his territory he had to pay the price in the form of his life. So we can say, what happened in his life should have been a part of his destiny only.

We may amend our destiny only if somebody could tell us about our destiny in advance.

Had it been possible to ascertain our destinies in advance palmists would have hogged the scene who were under the impression that they could predict destinies by seeing the palms of the people? But it all ended up in a flop show only. Numerologists also fell into the queue. Somehow they too could not keep their shops open much too long.

Today we know that we can get even our heart transplanted if it may fail. We can get even our kidney or liver transplanted if we have the money we may have to pay for such transplantation. But sometimes even if we have plenty of money we may not get any reprieve.

So we realize that life is only a 'Hide and seek' game we play with our destiny. At times we hide and our destiny finds out our hideout. Sometimes our destiny hides and we find out its hideout.

# 6

## Shall We Move Out to a New Star System in 3797?

Baba Vanga was born Vangelia Pandeva Dimitrova in Strumica, a village located at the foot of a volcanic mountain range in the Republic of Macedonia what was then the Ottoman Empire, in the year 1911.

According to folklore, she led an ordinary life up until the age of 12, when she mysteriously lost her eyesight during a massive storm — described by some as a freak tornado because she had been flung into the air by the tornado to have dashed to the ground from quite a height.

What happened next is murky but her family reportedly found her in a terrible state several days later, her injured eyes sealed shut and encrusted with a thick layer of dust and dirt. Too poor to afford specialist care, she was relegated to a life of blindness.

Vanga later stated that she had experienced her first vision during the days she was missing and believed she had been instilled with the ability to heal people and predict the future. She was able to convince others of her paranormal powers and quickly developed a cult following. She became the go-to psychic for the rich and powerful and admirers, among them heads of state, scientists and historians, would come from all over the world for a few minutes in her company.

She later served as an adviser to Bulgarian Communist Party leaders, some of whom allegedly exploited her gift to further their own agendas. She was reportedly kept under surveillance by the country's secret service and her home, the scene of countless meetings with visiting foreign politician and businessmen, reported bugged.

According to her prophesies Muslims will invade Europe in 2016. The Europe will cease to exist as we know it and the ensuing campaign of destruction will last years. The populations would be driven out and the entire continent would become almost empty. Though any such thing may not happen if we look at the stern stance taken by the US, Russia and Britain since some of her earlier prophesies have already surprised us we may not be able to say much about her this prophesy. Time alone will tell us.

Similarly she has also prophesied that the earth's orbit will change in 2023 and the population of Europe will reach almost zero in 2025.

She has prophesied that mankind will fly to Venus in hope of finding new sources of energy in 2028 and world water levels will rise as the polar ice caps melt in 2033.

According to her prophesies Europe will get transformed into an Islamic caliphate completely and Rome would be named its capital and the world's economy would thrive under Muslim rule in 2043.

Though we may not live up to 2043 to see whether her prophesy would fall flat or would come out true, the war going on in Syria has roused interest in her prophesies.

If that sounds dramatic, consider the developments of the past year, which has seen ISIS edge perilously close to Europe with the taking of Sirte, a key Libyan city overlooking the Mediterranean and the birthplace of the late dictator Gaddafi.

Sirte is now an Islamic State colony operating under Sharia Law. The new regime reportedly cemented its authority by staging a series of public executions, during which an unknown number of people were crucified and beheaded.

ISIS continues to gain ground in Syria, despite a massive bombing campaign by allied forces in the wake of the Paris attacks.

She has predicted that America will use a new climate change weapon for the first time in a bid to retake Rome and would bring back Christianity in 2066 but Communism will return to Europe and the rest of the world in 2076.

She has prophesied that Man-made sun will illuminate the dark side of the planet in 2100. Since scientists have been working on creating an artificial sun using nuclear fusion technology since 2008, her prophesy may quite come out true.

Though it may surprise all of us, she has prophesied that aliens will help the civilisations to live underwater in 2130. If this may so happen, it would lend credibility to the belief that Homo sapiens may have arrived on the earth from some star only.

She has also prophesied that the world would witness a major global drought in 2170. Hindus call it *Jal Pralaya*. Though ice caps have started melting due to global warming presumably due to rapid industrialization, we should not get surprised if a large portion of Earth gets deluged within next 154 years as predicted by her because though last century's average rate of rise in sea level was 1.7 millimetres per year according to satellite altimetry data the sea level is rising at a faster rate year by year by as much as 3 millimetres per year, unless some wise steps are taken by all countries well within time.

Of course our scientists may possibly be able to stop two large volcanic eruptions successfully in 2187 as prophesied by her.

She has gone beyond 2187 by predicting that temperatures would drop in 2201 as the sun's thermonuclear processes slow down. Planets will slowly change orbits in 2262 and Mars will be threatened by a comet and an accident on the artificial sun will result in more drought in 2354.

She has also prophesied that two artificial suns will collide and leave the Earth in the dark in 2480 and that a war on Mars will change its trajectory in 3005.

She has also prophesied that the mankind would face a crisis since a comet will hit the moon due to which the Earth will get surrounded by a ring of rock and ash in 3010 and by 3797 everything on the Earth will die. But human civilisation would have advanced so much that it would be able to move to a new star system.

Though we would not be alive till 3797 to see whether people would shift to some other star system or not through the year 3797 as predicted by her but all the while the life of our planet does not seem to be quite as short as she had predicted. But if her predictions for the years 2016 and 2023 may turn out to be true we would have to take her other predictions also seriously.

We can of course wait and watch till 2023 at least.

So far as our going to some star, that too some new star is concerned it makes us suspicious of her prophesies. But we need not be suspicious simply on this count. So far as my mind goes, we know that some hotels are being planned to be constructed in the outer space. It is possible that some people may go to live in such of the hotels or may start living in a colony on some planet in 3797 and she may have envisioned such a chain of illuminated hotels or colonies only as a new star system.

You may be amazed but she had predicted that the 44th president of the United States would be African American. But she had also stated that he would be the "last US president". Since we'll be able to probably see in our own life how this prediction pans out we shall be able to make an opinion about the possibilities of somebody's ability to see the future to predict what may or may not happen in the world only when we find out whether her other prophesies also come out true or not.

The same way there may not be total destruction in 3797 either. Vanga may have seen only a large-scale destruction that may have appeared to her as something resembling total destruction. Of course time alone would tell which of her prophesies are going to come out in full colours.

However, do you think science would ever be able to explain how somebody may at all be able to look into the future as vividly as she was able to look?

Perhaps never and we also know the reason, why. Science would be able to do little to tell us anything about such a possibility because according to it, everything has to be either animate or inanimate but God is neither animate nor inanimate as has been explained in the second chapter of the book.

Although anybody may have intuitions or premonitions but we cannot prophesise like her. Though prophesies may appear to be akin to intuitions or premonitions, in strict sense it is perhaps not so. Intuitions and premonitions are based on some prior information that may have already got registered in our mind in the past. For instance take the case of a robber who may be planning to rob a bank having a premonition or intuition that he may get caught by the police. He would have not had such an intuition or such premonition had he not known what he may have been planning to do. Anybody can guess the possible consequences because he knows what he has been planning to do or what he may be all about to do. Intuitions and premonitions come out of only what may be already hidden in our subconscious mind. But our subconscious mind does not hide anything that may help us to make prophesies.

Do you think somebody may have been sending some sort of silent messages from somewhere to tell her what was going to happen in the future? Only such person could have sent such messages who would have known what was going to happen in the future. Whom do you think would ever know what was going to happen in the future?

Future certainly does not depend only on what we may be planning. It also depends on what others may be planning. How may we ever know who would be planning what?

What difference would it have made even if we had known who was going to plan what? One does not have to be a mathematician to predict the future for Vanga was not literate enough to have learnt mathematics.

So, on the face of it, how people must be making predictions is a mystery only.

In an attempt to decipher this mystery we may only say, since we couldn't have created the Universe we presumed that God must have created the Universe. Likewise we also assumed that God must have created all the fauna and flora since we couldn't have created such a large variety of fauna and flora.

The same way we may add one more line to our presumptions that God alone may be knowing, what was going to happen in the future and the people who may be prophesising may be simply getting ON LINE with Him while prophesising. If we may also learn the art of getting ON LINE with Him, who knows, we may also be able to prophesise like Baba Vanga.

Of course at this point it is quite natural to think what if the prophesies of Baba Vanga fall flat? Atheists would certainly wish her prophesies to fall flat. Though not certain, if not all, no one knows some of her prophesies may fall flat. A question arises in that case, would it justify the stand of the atheists? It is obviously not possible to answer this question straight away. Only time would testify the truth of her prophesies. True picture will emerge in 3797 only. We have to wait till then to arrive at any concrete conclusion.

# 7

## The Feedback Systems of God

Is it not really awesome that though we are still in the primitive stage of developing artificial suns, God should have been able to have evolved so many suns so many years back using the very technology of nuclear fusion we are planning to use to construct artificial suns? It is really awesome to even think of the immense capabilities of the God who may have created the Universe.

The way a child does not know who his father may have been we also don't know who the Creator of the Universe may have been but it does not straight away imply that the Universe may have come into existence all by itself.

When we come across a poem we may not know who may have written it but it does not connote that nobody must have written the poem. The same way we can't connote that nobody may have evolved the Universe.

Do you still have a doubt whether He exists or not?

We don't have to doubt whether God exists or not. We should take it for granted that there has to be some super genius Entity that ought to have created the Universe, the Universe to which the solar system to which our earth belongs, belongs. We would have not been there had the Universe not been there. So it is this very Creator whom we owe our existence.

We would have not been on the earth had this earth not been there. Nor this earth would have been there had our solar system not been there. We thus owe our very existence to that Supreme God, who ought to have created the Universe.

We may be just a speck of the Universe but we owe our existence not only to our parents but to Him also.

The way a poet keeps on writing new poems, a painter keeps on painting new paintings, a sculptor keeps on sculpting new sculptures and an author keeps on writing new books, it appears God is fond of creating solar systems in the Universe and if it were to have been so, it is also quite logical to assume that He too must be not simply loving the solar systems created by Him the same way as a poet loves the poems written by him or a painter loves the paintings made by him and a sculptor the sculptures sculpted by him but must be also keeping a track of what shape the Universe created by Him may have taken through all so many years. It is not possible that He may not be keeping a constant eye on what is going on in His Universe.

If we can be so careful about our creations do you think God would have gone on a holiday after creating the Universe without having evolved any feedback systems?

No. He too must be having the like of CCTV cameras we have developed for ourselves, to keep a tab on everything that may be happening in the Universe. He too ought to have developed a perfect system of continuous feedback to get abreast of everything that may be happening in the Universe. Don't you think so?

It would be foolish to doubt whether He could have had the capability of evolving necessary Feed Back systems for Himself or not. If He could have created the Universe it would have been possible for Him to have evolved a feedback system as well.

In fact, we should bow our head to the God also the way we bow our head to our father. We need not doubt His existence. He could as well be very much around us very close to us to watch us or be watching our all activities through His CCTV cameras. We may not be aware of His CCTV cameras but He ought to have installed such cameras everywhere in the Universe to have a continuous feedback. He may be getting not only a feedback of what may be happening around us but everything that may be happening anywhere in the whole Universe to be God.

# 8

## Views of Kyle Butt on Existence of God

Kyle Butt has come out very beautifully on the riddle surrounding the existence of God in his article "Cause and Effect - Scientific Proof that God Exists". In this article he dispels the doubts on existence of God by giving the logic of Cause and Effect. The article originally published by Apologetics Press tells why we should not have any doubts on the existence of God.

The article[1] sourced from the site http://www.apologeticspress. org is being reproduced here in italics which makes a must read for everyone.

*Every rational person must admit "The Universe exists and is real". If it did not exist, we would not be here to talk about it. So the question arises, "How did the Universe get here?" Did it create itself? If it did not create itself, it must have had a cause.*

*Let's look at the law of cause and effect. As far as science knows, natural laws have no exceptions. This is definitely true of the law of cause and effect, which is the most universal and most certain of all laws. Simply put, the law of cause and effect states that every material effect must have an adequate cause that existed before the effect.*

*Material effects without adequate causes do not exist. Also, causes never occur after the effect. In addition, the effect never is greater than the cause. That is why scientists say that every material effect must have an adequate cause. The river did not turn muddy because the frog jumped in; the book did not fall off the table because the fly landed on it. These are not adequate causes. For whatever effects we see, we must present adequate causes.*

*Five-year-olds are wonderful at using the law of cause and effect. We can picture a small child asking: "Mommy, where do peaches come from?" His mother says that they come from peach trees. Then the child asks where the trees come from, and his mother explains that they come from peaches. You can see the cycle. Eventually the child wants to know how the first peach tree got here. He can see very well that it must have had a cause, and he wants to know what that cause was.*

*One thing is for sure: the Universe did not create itself! We know this for a scientific fact, because matter cannot create matter. If we take a rock that weighs 1 pound and do 50,000 experiments on it, we never will be able to produce more than 1 pound of rock. So, whatever caused the Universe could not have been material.*

## FROM NOTHING COMES NOTHING

*I know that it is insulting to your intelligence to have to include this paragraph, but some people today are saying that the Universe evolved from nothing. However, if there ever had been a time when absolutely nothing existed, then there would be nothing now, because it always is true that nothing produces nothing. If something exists now, then something always has existed.*

*Only God fits the criteria of an adequate cause that came before the Universe.*

## WHY DOES GOD NOT HAVE A CAUSE?

*Hold on just a minute! If we contend that every material effect must have a cause, and we say that only God could have caused the Universe, then the obvious question is: "What caused God?" Doesn't the law of cause and effect apply to God, too?*

*There is a single word in the law of cause and effect that helps provide the answer to this question—the word material. Every material effect must have a cause that existed before it. Scientists formulated the law of cause and effect based upon what they have observed while studying this Universe, which is made out of matter. No science experiment in the world can be performed on God, because He is an eternal spirit, not matter (John 4:24). Science is far from learning everything about this material world and it is even farther from understanding the eternal nature of God. There had to be a First Cause, and God was (and is) the only One suitable for the job.*

## CONCLUSION

*The law of cause and effect is a well-established law that does not have any known exceptions. It was not conjured up from the creationists' magic hat to prove the existence of God (although it does that quite well). The evidence is sufficient to show that this material Universe needs a non-material cause. That non-material Cause is God. If natural forces created the Universe, randomly selecting themselves then morality in humans never could be explained.*

---

1 Reproduced with the permission of the publisher Apologetics Press

# 9

## Story of Natalya Demkina -The X-Ray Girl[1]

*Born Natalya Nikolayevna Demkina in Saransk, western Russia, in 1987, this paranormal talent claims to be able to make medical diagnoses by using special vision. It is reported that the "X-ray Girl", as she was nicknamed by the Russian tabloid newspaper Pravda, is able to see organs and tissues inside human bodies and discover medical ailments the person may be suffering from. Since the age of ten, after an operation to have her appendix removed, Natalya (also known as Natasha) has been making accurate medical readings in Russia, in her own words:*

*"For a fraction of a second, I see a colorful picture inside the person and then I start to analyze it."*

*Natalya's abilities were tested by doctors at a children's hospital in her home town, where she was reported to have correctly diagnosed the illnesses of several patients, including one of the doctors.*

*After using her special vision to examine the patients, sometimes down to molecular level, Natalya is said to have drawn pictures of what she saw inside their bodies. She also apparently corrected a misdiagnosis made by a doctor at the hospital on a female patient who was told she had cancer. When Natalya examined the woman she only saw a small cyst. Secondary examination revealed that Natasha had been right and the woman did not have cancer.*

*After the news of Natalya's incredible ability spread, the story was picked up in 2003 by a local newspaper and TV station, and eventually by British tabloid newspaper The Sun. This newspaper brought Natalya to England in January 2004, where she allegedly demonstrated her diagnostic powers successfully on Sun reporter Briony Warden, who had received multiple injuries after being hit by a car the previous October. While in England Natalya also examined resident medic of the This Morning T.V. show* Doctor Chris, initially making correct identifications of previous medical operations he had undergone, and then *stating that the Doctor was suffering from various ailments including "gall stones, kidney stones, and enlarged liver and an enlarged pancreas". Somewhat shaken, Dr Chris underwent a scan at a local hospital to discover how accurate Natalya's diagnosis had been. He discovered that although the scan did show a possible tumour in his intestines there were no serious health problems.*

*The best known and most controversial test performed on the X-Ray Girl's paranormal powers was that organized by the Discovery Channel in New York in May 2004. The test, which was part of a Discovery Channel documentary entitled The Girl with X-Ray Eyes, was carried out by researchers Ray Hyman and Richard Wiseman from the Committee for Skeptical Inquiry (CSI) and Andrew Skolnick of the Commission for Scientific Medicine and Mental Health (CSMMH). The 4-hour long investigation involved seven test persons, one of whom was a normal control subject. Natalya was given seven diagnoses written by doctors and was required to match at least five of these to the corresponding patient in order to prove that her abilities were unusual enough to warrant further testing. In the event Demkina was able to match only four of the seven correctly and thus the researchers concluded that she had failed the test and left it at that.*

*But matters were not to be so straight forward. Acrimonious disputes arose between Natalya's supporters, who believed she had been unfairly dealt with, and the investigators. Demkina herself was extremely critical of the conditions under which she had been tested and the way in which she was treated. The research team responded by asking why Demkina had been unable to detect a metal plate inside one subject's head, especially as its outline was visible beneath the person's skull.*

*However, Nobel Prize-winning physicist and the director of University of Cambridge's Mind-Matter Unification project, Brian Josephson, has also added his voice to the criticism of the tests carried out in New York. Josephson is of the opinion that the tests were set up to discredit Demkina, and that the odds of Demkina managing four matches from seven by chance alone would be 1 in 50.*

*He believes that the results from the Demkina experiment should have been classed as "inconclusive".*

*Demkina's New York experiment remains controversial to this day and is still the subject of heated debate on internet science and paranormal forums. But there are two points which are worth bearing in mind, the first of which is that before the New York test Demkina had claimed that she would be 100% correct in her diagnoses, which was obviously not the case. Secondly, she had also agreed to rules which stated that to pass the test she would have to correctly match at least five of the diagnoses with the corresponding patients. For her complaints to have any validity, they should have been made before the tests not after.*

Though unarguably both the points seem to be very valid points all right because the team had explained these anomalies to Natasha through her translator and had set a target that she should be able to tell correctly who had which anomaly for as many as at least five anomalies, to qualify but look at the choice of the anomalies of the people they had selected for conducting the test, they had made.

While one of them did not have any anomaly the others had following anomalies in their bodies.

(i) One of them had metal surgical staples in his chest from open heart surgery.

(ii) One of them had a section of her esophagus surgically removed.

(iii) One of them had a large section of one lung removed.

(iv) One of them had an artificial hip replacement.

(v) One of them had a missing appendix (Though later on it was found that one more person also had a missing appendix).

(vi) One of them had a large brain tumor removed due to which he had a large hole in his skull covered by a metal plate.

Just to check whether she could have seen through the human body or not, should such a rigorous choice of anomalies have been at all necessary?

The choice of the anomalies itself makes one suspicious that they must have been pretty well pre-biased that no one may see through the human bodies with bare eyes.

The choice made by them itself leads one to doubt that they should have been loaded with scepticism ahead of their conducting the test.

However the aspersions raised by Brian Josephson on the evaluation methods used by CSICOP and CSMMH at New York prompted Professor Yoshio Machi of the Department of Electronics at Tokyo Denki University to give Demkina one more chance by inviting her to Japan to prove to the world whether she had the ability of seeing the inner organs of the people through bare eyes or not.

*After the inconclusive nature of the U.K and New York tests Natalya travelled to Tokyo, Japan, where she underwent experiments with Professor Yoshio Machi, Demkina stipulated beforehand that she would only be tested under certain conditions, which included that each patient brought with them a medical certificate stating the condition of their health, and that her diagnoses were to be limited to a single specific part of the body - the head, the trunk, or extremities. The teenager also insisted that she was to be told in advance which part of the body she was to examine. According to the website Pravda.ru the tests were successful, with Natasha able to see that one of the patients had a prosthetic knee, and another had asymmetrically placed internal organs. She was even able to diagnose the early stages of pregnancy in a female patient.*

*However, practically all the information for the Tokyo tests comes either from Demkina's own website or from the Pravda. ru website, the latter hardly a reliable source. Critics point out that, as with Demkina's tests in England, the Tokyo experiments were not performed under strict conditions nor were they subject to independent review.*

Sceptics may be right but do you think science or medicine would be ever able to explain such a possibility?

We don't have to go too far in search of an answer, however.

We have to only look back at one more equally amazing case, the case of Shakuntala Devi. No normal person could calculate at the speed of a supercomputer as she could. It is well known that she had amazed everyone by calculating the 23rd root of a 201-digit number just in 50 seconds in 1977 at Southern Methodist University and her answer—546,372,891—was confirmed by calculations done at the US Bureau of Standards by the

UNIVAC 1101 computer, for which a special program had to be written to perform such a large calculation or by multiplying two 13-digit numbers—7,686,369,774,870 and 2,465,099,745,779—picked at random by the Computer Department of Imperial College London in 1980 by giving a correct answer - 18,947,668,177,995,426,462,773,730 - in 28 seconds – a record that could find an entry in the 1982 *Guinness Book of Records* or by calculating the cube root of 61,629,875 and the seventh root of 170,859,375 (395 and 15, respectively) even before Arthur Jensen, the professor of psychology at the University of California, Berkeley, who had tested her mathematical skills when she had gone to US in 1988 even before he could have copied down the numbers in his notebook.

Only the famished life Shakuntala Devi had led during childhood could have had an impact on the mathematical circuits of her brain, what else?

Both Shakuntala Devi and Natasha Demkina have one thing in common. The both had quite insalubrious childhood and it looks such events of their life may have been behind such a metamorphosis of their brains.

In case of Natasha Demkina for instance we know, she had undergone an appendicitis operation in her childhood. When she was discharged by the hospital after removal of her appendix she was not able to straighten up because the doctors had forgotten to remove a swab from her intestinal cavity. Since she had developed such vision after the doctors put her back on the operating table and removed the sutures her parents believe that this operation could have had some semblance for her such capability.

But do you think acquisition of X–ray vision and a surgical operation may not ever have any semblance? At least I do not think so.

According to me our eyes do not work in isolation. They connect us with the world through the vision-related circuits of our brain. We are able to recognise whatever our eyes see, through these circuits only. We may have normal vision only as long as these circuits do not get re-spliced.

So let us believe, the vision-circuits of the brain of Natalya Demkina must have undergone a radical change when the swab had been removed from her intestinal cavity so as to have enabled her to see the inner organs of the human bodies much the same way as the mathematical circuits of Shakuntala Devi's brain ought to have undergone during her childhood to have let her brain work like a supercomputer. If we don't doubt that Shakuntala Devi's brain had the capability of working just like a supercomputer why should we be so reluctant to submit to the possibility of Natalya Demkina's brain doubling up like an X-Ray Machine?

God should have certainly thought of the type of problems that could have arisen had He provided everyone the vision-circuits that would have allowed us to see through the bodies of others like Natalya Demkina. It ought to have been quite a task to finalize the default vision-circuits. Who must have finalized the type of default circuits we ought to have had? Obviously not we, the humans! Who else do you think? Do we not get a hint? It could have been only God, none else?

Such cases stand a testimony to the existence of God. Any doubts?

---

1 Reproduced the italicized portion of this chapter with the permission of the author Brian Haughton from the web site http://www.mysteriouspeople.com/Natalya_Demkina.htm

# 10

## Views of Marilyn Adamson on Existence of God

To believe in God or not, basically depends on whether we are willing to believe what stands out on logic even though we may not have a veritable proof lined up to convince us or not.

Marilyn Adamson found it difficult to refute the continuously answered prayers and quality of life of a close friend. In challenging the beliefs of her friend, Marilyn got amazed to learn the wealth of objective evidence pointing to the existence of God. After about a year of persistent questioning, she responded to God's offer to come into her life and substantiated the existence of God in an article "Is There a God?" by giving six captivating reasons for us to believe why we should not doubt His existence.

The logic given by her is so compelling that once you read this article you would not look for any proof. The main reason that prevents science to establish the existence of God lies in its basic concept of looking for a proof rather

S C Sawhney

than logic. We can believe in the existence of God only if we understand that everything does not call for a proof if we get satisfied by the logic put forth by someone.

You can see it for yourself through this article[1], which is being reproduced here solely with this purpose only. She has moved around the topic of God in the following manner.

## 1. Does God exist? The complexity of our planet points to a deliberate Designer who not only created our universe, but sustains it today.

*Many examples showing God's design could be given, possibly with no end. But here are a few:*

*The Earth...its size is perfect. The Earth's size and corresponding gravity holds a thin layer of mostly nitrogen and oxygen gases, only extending about 50 miles above the Earth's surface. If Earth were smaller, an atmosphere would be impossible, like the planet Mercury. If Earth were larger, its atmosphere would contain free hydrogen, like Jupiter. Earth is the only known planet equipped with an atmosphere of the right mixture of gases to sustain plant, animal and human life.*

*The Earth is located the right distance from the sun. Consider the temperature swings we encounter, roughly -30 degrees to +120 degrees. If the Earth were any further away from the sun, we would all freeze. Any closer and we would burn up. Even a fractional variance in the Earth's position to the sun would make life on Earth impossible. The Earth remains this perfect distance from the sun while it rotates around the sun at a speed of nearly 67,000 mph. It is also rotating on its axis, allowing the entire surface of the Earth to be properly warmed and cooled every day.*

*And our moon is the perfect size and distance from the Earth for its gravitational pull. The moon creates important ocean tides and movement so ocean waters do not stagnate, and yet our massive oceans are restrained from spilling over across the continents.*

***Water****... colorless, odorless and without taste, and yet no living thing can survive without it. Plants, animals and human beings consist mostly of water (about two-thirds of the human body is water). You'll see why the characteristics of water are uniquely suited to life:*

*It has wide margin between its boiling point and freezing point. Water allows us to live in an environment of fluctuating temperature changes, while keeping our bodies a steady 98.6 degrees.*

*Water is a universal solvent. This property of water means that various chemicals, minerals and nutrients can be carried throughout our bodies and into the smallest blood vessels.*

*Water is also chemically neutral. Without affecting the makeup of the substances it carries, water enables food, medicines and minerals to be absorbed and used by the body.*

*Water has a unique surface tension. Water in plants can therefore flow upward against gravity, bringing life-giving water and nutrients to the top of even the tallest trees.*

*Water freezes from the top down and floats, so fish can live in the winter.*

*Ninety-seven percent of the Earth's water is in the oceans. But on our Earth, there is a system designed which removes salt from the water and then distributes that water throughout the globe. Evaporation takes the ocean waters, leaving the salt, and forms clouds which are easily moved by the wind to disperse water over the land, for vegetation, animals and people. It is a system of purification and supply that sustains life on this planet, a system of recycled and reused water.*

***The human brain...*** *simultaneously processes an amazing amount of information. Your brain takes in all the colors and objects you see, the temperature around you, the pressure of your feet against the floor, the sounds around you, the dryness of your mouth, even the texture of your keyboard. Your brain holds and processes all your emotions, thoughts and memories. At the same time your brain keeps track of the ongoing functions of your body like your breathing pattern, eyelid movement, hunger and movement of the muscles in your hands.*

*The human brain processes more than a million messages a second. Your brain weighs the importance of all this data, filtering out the relatively unimportant. This screening function is what allows you to focus and operate effectively in your world. The brain functions differently than other organs. There is an intelligence to it, the ability to reason, to produce feelings, to dream and plan, to take action, and relate to other people.*

***The eye...*** *can distinguish among seven million colors. It has automatic focusing and handles an astounding 1.5 million* *messages -- simultaneously. Evolution focuses on mutations and changes from and within existing organisms. Yet evolution alone does not fully explain the initial source of the eye or the brain -- the start of living organisms from nonliving matter.*

## 2. Does God exist? The universe had a start - what caused it?

*Scientists are convinced that our universe began with one enormous explosion of energy and light, which we now call the Big Bang. This was the singular start to everything that exists: the beginning of the universe, the start of space, and even the initial start of time itself.*

*Astrophysicist Robert Jastrow, a self-described agnostic, stated, "The seed of everything that has happened in the Universe was planted in that first instant; every star, every planet and every living creature in the Universe came into being as a result of events that were set in motion in the moment of the cosmic explosion... The Universe flashed into being, and we cannot find out what caused that to happen."*

*Steven Weinberg, a Nobel laureate in Physics, said at the moment of this explosion, "the universe was about a hundred thousands million degrees Centigrade... and the universe was filled with light."*

*The universe has not always existed. It had a start... what caused that? Scientists have no explanation for the sudden explosion of light and matter.*

### 3. Does God exist? The universe operates by uniform laws of nature. Why does it?

*Much of life may seem uncertain, but look at what we can count on day after day: gravity remains consistent, a hot cup of coffee left on a counter will get cold, the earth rotates in the same 24 hours, and the speed of light doesn't change -- on earth or in galaxies far from us.*

*How is it that we can identify laws of nature that never change? Why is the universe so orderly, so reliable?*

*"The greatest scientists have been struck by how strange this is. There is no logical necessity for a universe that obeys rules, let alone one that abides by the rules of mathematics. This astonishment springs from the recognition that the universe doesn't have to behave this way. It is easy to imagine a universe in which conditions change unpredictably from instant to instant, or even a universe in which things pop in and out of existence."*

*Richard Feynman, a Nobel Prize winner for quantum electrodynamics, said, "Why nature is mathematical is a mystery... The fact that there are rules at all is a kind of miracle."*

## 4. Does God exist? The DNA code informs, programs a cell's behavior.

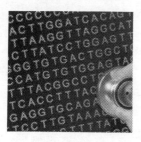 *All instruction, all teaching, all training comes with intent. Someone who writes an instruction manual does so with purpose. Did you know that in every cell of our bodies there exists a very detailed instruction code, much like a miniature computer program?*

*As you may know, a computer program is made up of ones and zeros, like this: 110010101011000. The way they are arranged tell the computer program what to do. The dna code in each of our cells is very similar. It's made up of four chemicals that scientists abbreviate as a, t, g, and c. These are arranged in the human cell like this: cgtgtgactcgctcctgat and so on. There are three billion of these letters in every human cell!!*

*Well, just like you can program your phone to beep for specific reasons, dna instructs the cell. Dna is a three-billion-lettered program telling the cell to act in a certain way. It is a full instruction manual.*

*Why is this so amazing? One has to ask.... how did this information program wind up in each human cell? These are not just chemicals. These are chemicals that instruct, that code in a very detailed way exactly how the person's body should develop.*

*Natural, biological causes are completely lacking as an explanation when programmed information is involved. You cannot find instruction, precise information like this, without someone intentionally constructing it.*

We may of course say that to do anything we need basic intelligence. Of course we may argue, "The very fact that evolution of the Universe and evolution of all flora and fauna should have required enormous intelligence far more than human intelligence strongly hints at the existence of Someone who should have been way ahead all of us in His intelligence" and justify the existence of God on this basis but it may be even otherwise if we go by the following argument.

No doubt we could not convert iron or lead into gold during the Alchemists' era. But in that era we could have not engineered the atoms. Today we have been able to produce more than 24 synthetic elements, Ununseptium having atomic number 117 being the latest one having been synthesized only as recently as in year 2010. Though some of the 94 elements had been also created synthetically but were later on found to also exist in nature.

We may of course argue that all the naturally found 48 elements that came into existence could have very well come into existence due to the natural process of cooling down of the Earth through the time of its inception itself. It did not call for any special intelligence. Though it may definitely bring a smile on the faces of the atheists but actually what could have been true of these elements could have not been true of the existence of the dna codes.

So eventually we end up in the lap of theism only.

## 5. Does God exist? We know God exists because he pursues us. He is constantly initiating and seeking for us to come to him.

*I was an atheist at one time. And like many atheists, the issue of people believing in God bothered me greatly. What is it about atheists that we would spend so much time, attention, and energy refuting something that we don't believe even exists? What causes us to do that? When I was an atheist, I attributed my intentions as caring for those poor, delusional people... to help them realize their hope was completely ill-founded. To be honest, I also had another motive. As I challenged those who believed in God, I was deeply curious to see if they could convince me otherwise. Part of my quest was to become free from the question of God. If I could conclusively prove to believers that they were wrong, then the issue is off the table, and I would be free to go about my life.*

*I didn't realize that the reason the topic of God weighed so heavily on my mind, was because God was pressing the issue. I have come to find out that God wants to be known. He created us with the intention that we would know him. He has surrounded us with evidence of himself and he keeps the question of his existence squarely before us. It was as if I couldn't escape thinking about the possibility of God. In fact, the day I chose to acknowledge God's existence, my prayer began with, "Ok, you win..." It might be that the underlying reason atheists are bothered by people believing in God is because God is actively pursuing them.*

*I am not the only one who has experienced this. Malcolm Muggeridge, socialist and philosophical author, wrote, "I had a notion that somehow, besides questing, I was being pursued." C.S. Lewis said he remembered, "...night after night, feeling whenever my mind lifted even for a second from my work, the steady, unrelenting approach of Him whom I so earnestly desired not to meet. I gave in, and admitted that God was God, and knelt and prayed: perhaps, that night, the most dejected and reluctant convert in all of England."*

*Lewis went on to write a book titled, "Surprised by Joy" as a result of knowing God. I too had no expectations other than rightfully admitting God's existence. Yet over the following several months, I became amazed by his love for me.*

## 6. Does God exist? Unlike any other revelation of God, Jesus Christ is the clearest, most specific picture of God revealing himself to us.

*Why Jesus? Look throughout the major world religions and you'll find that Buddha, Muhammad, Confucius and Moses all identified themselves as teachers or prophets. None of them ever claimed to be equal to God. Surprisingly, Jesus did. That is what sets Jesus apart from all the others. He said God exists and you're looking at him. Though he talked about his Father in heaven, it was not from the position of separation, but of very close union, unique to all humankind. Jesus said that anyone who had seen Him had seen the Father, anyone who believed in him, believed in the Father.*

*He said, "I am the light of the world, he who follows me will not walk in darkness, but will have the light of life." He claimed attributes belonging only to God: to be able to forgive people of their sin, free them from habits of sin, give people a more abundant life and give them eternal life in heaven. Unlike other teachers who focused people on their words, Jesus pointed people to himself. He did not say, "follow my words and you will find truth." He said, "I am the way, the truth, and the life, no one comes to the Father but through me."*

However sadly, she seems to have erred here a little bit. She is not wrong in mentioning that Buddha had not identified himself as God as Jesus had done but he did not identify himself as God since he very well knew that he was not God. But we should not forget that Vedas had been quite specific to mention that God is beyond our consciousness and we can see Him only if we go beyond the veil of consciousness. If she would have found out what Vedas have to tell us about God perhaps she would have admitted that Vedas also expect us to lead as righteous a life as had Jesus prompted the people at his gatherings.

## *If you want to begin a relationship with God now, you can.*

*This is your decision, no coercion here. But if you want to be forgiven by God and come into a relationship with him, you can do so right now by asking him to forgive you and come into your life. Jesus said, "Behold, I stand at the door [of your heart] and knock. He who hears my voice and opens the door, I will come into him [or her]." If you want to do this, but aren't sure how to put it into words, this may help: "Jesus, thank you for dying for my sins. You know my life and that I need to be forgiven. I ask you to forgive me right now and come into my life. I want to know you in a real way. Come into my life now. Thank you that you wanted a relationship with me. Amen."*

*God views your relationship with him as permanent. Referring to all those who believe in him, Jesus Christ said of us, "I know them, and they follow me; and I give them eternal life, and they shall never perish, and no one shall snatch them out of my hand."*

*Looking at all these facts, one can conclude that a loving God does exist and can be known in an intimate, personal way.*

Why should God have to come down from the heavens to convince us whether He exists or not? We have to find out ourselves whether He exists or not.

We are not able to see Him only because, who knows, He may still be in the same form of dark energy or dark matter (or Baryonic matter) in which He may have been when He should have engineered Big Bangs to create the Universe.

---

1 Sourced from the website www.EveryStudent.com with the permission of the author , Marilyn Adamson

# 11

## Views of Steve Moxham on Existence of God

Steve Moxham has given a revealing proof of the existence of God in his message[1] "I Have Communicated with the God" posted at his website http://www.stevemoxham.com on 13th December, 2015.

In this message he claims to have communicated with God personally and directly. Surely it makes an interesting study on the topic of existence of God. The message given by him is reproduced here in italics.

*While lying in bed, not thinking about anything, I suddenly felt the Spirit of God come upon me and I immediately knew what God wanted me to do. He wanted me to ask him a question about how much my business was worth to a NASDAQ company which tried to acquire my website business over a year earlier. So I did.*

*I prayed to God and asked Him how much my website business was worth to Internet Brands, Inc. I started at US$550,000* *and went up in $100,000 increments until He stopped me at US$1,250,000 or US$1250k. When He stopped me at US$1250k ($1.25 million) it was like hitting a brick wall! There was no further room to go, either up, down or sideways!*

*Ironically, the time that the last email arrived from them was at 12:50PM - the exact number which God had let me know my website was worth to them! $1250K.*

*This was my first experience of communicating directly with God and it was an interesting one to say the least!*

*People say that they 'hear' the voice of God, but this was not any voice or words. It was all done in the Spirit of God where He hears your inner thoughts and voice!*

*So getting back to my original point about proving the existence of God, I'll have to draw your attention to the valuation document which I created for "Internet Brands, Inc" over a year earlier before this all happened.*

*In that valuation document I calculated that my website would add approximately US$2.5 million to Internet Brands's overall market value listed on the NASDAQ Stock Exchange in America. It wasn't until several months after talking with God that I went back to this valuation document and saw that I had calculated that my website would have added US$2.5 million to their overall market value, and that the US$1.25 million that God had told me that my website was worth to them was exactly half the value that I had calculated! That was an eye-opener!*

*So what does that mean? It means that if Internet Brands had offered me US$1.25 million for my website business, then they stood to double the value of their investment after purchasing it! So why did God wish to tell me that? Because it had a devastating impact on my life in that the people who were supposed to buy my website business at that time, did not, having only offered me US$400,000 - US$500,000 for the business. This represented 32-40% or 1/3rd to 2/5ths of God's valuation!*

*While that may not 'prove' God for many people, it is the only time I have ever had direct one-to-one feedback and communication with what many of us call 'God'!*

*So I can say hand-on-heart and without a shadow of a doubt that God exists and is real, and is ready to communicate with you too! All He asks is for an open heart and mind, and a willingness to believe in that which is unseen, but still real, and still exists today!*

---

1 Reproduced with the permission of the author

# 12

## True-to-Life Illusionary Visions

Have you ever met God? If not, how can you assert that God exists? If you think you had met God it may have been only an illusion because sometimes even illusions can appear to be true to life. In this article I have covered some instances of illusions which appeared to be real but were actually just illusions.

I am explaining how we get an illusion of having seen Gods. Actually even I have seen a God once. It was when my younger brother had come from Kanpur to our house at Lucknow to take our father and mother with him because my father wanted to go back to Kanpur instead of staying with us.

Since my father did not like to stay with us, I engaged a taxi to let my brother take back him to Kanpur along with my mother. But to my great surprise when the taxi drove away I not only saw a white apparition of Yamraj, the Hindu God of death mounted on a buffalo, standing right behind the taxi it even whispered to me slylily, "I have come to take your father with me but I would follow him right up to the house of your brother before I pick up him."

Since I did not want to get ridiculed for having seen such an apparition and what it had told me I did not tell about it to anyone till next day morning when my brother rang up me to break the news of my father's death.

Actually only a day back my father had given a strange reason for his inclination of going back to Kanpur. He had told me that he would not like to die at Lucknow because he did not expect even a small crowd to turn up here on his funeral while at Kanpur he could expect a crowd of thousands of people. So I thought, I must have seen the image of Yamraj only because what my father had told me must have bounced back in my mind.

I had seen Yamraj mounted on a buffalo surely only because I had heard during my childhood that God of death comes on a buffalo to pick up the soul whenever somebody dies. So my sighting a God on a buffalo was merely a replication of such a belief only. This incident sufficiently explains why we feel that we have seen Gods.

After all why people don't see Yamraj mounted on a buffalo in other countries? God of death has to be same all around the world, isn't? How there could be different Gods for different countries? Obviously the scenes of Gods rise in our mind only due to hallucination.

To substantiate this concept I may narrate one more incident of the same type that supports this view further.

I had once seen a flame bedecked with a garland of flowers hanging on the side of a saucer sailing across the skyline going toward the cremation ground of Lucknow from my car when I had stopped the car for a few minutes near the church of Christ Church College due to red signal at the main crossing of Hazarat Ganj a few years back. The flame as well the garland appeared so real that I could not believe my eyes for a moment. But immediately it struck me that my subconscious mind must have reproduced what one of my friends had told me how the souls of holy people go to heaven. I recalled that he had told me that their souls sail across the sky exactly in the same manner as I was seeing at that moment.

I could make out that my mind should have tried to remind me what my friend had told me about the departure of the holy souls.

But I winked in disbelief because I realized what I was seeing was merely a deceptive illusion.

The images of various Gods we see are also just illusions of this type only.

There is nothing much real about them.

# 13

## The Impressions of God Having Visited Us

Sometimes we think that God had visited us even though it may not be really so.

Here is an interesting sequence of events which had appeared in the August, 2015 issue of the booklet "Chhoti Chhoti Batein" published by Source Publishers Pvt. Ltd., Mumbai that led a man to think that God had visited him. The story[1] "A Hot Cup of Tea" is being reproduced here due to its relevance to the theme of the book.

The story relates to a group of fifteen soldiers led by a Major who were on their way to the post in Himalayans where they were going to be deployed for the next three months. The batch that was going to be relieved waited anxiously for them.

*It was cold winter and intermittent snowfall made the treacherous climb cumbersome.*

They wished that someone could offer them a cup of tea but the Major thought it was very unlikely to get such help.

They continued for an hour or so till they came across a dilapidated structure, which looked like a tea shop but was locked, as it was well past midnight.

"No tea boys, bad luck", said the Major. But he suggested they all take some rest since they had been walking for over three hours. "Sir, this is a tea shop and we can make tea... We will have to break the lock", suggested one of the soldiers.

The officer was in great dilemma to the unethical suggestion, but the thought of a steaming cup of tea for the tired soldiers made him give the permission.

They were lucky as the place had everything they needed to make tea and also packets of biscuits. The soldiers took the tea and biscuits and got ready for the remaining journey.

The Major felt bad that they had to break the lock to take tea and biscuits without permission of the owner. Since they were not a band of thieves but disciplined soldiers, he took out a Rs 1000 note from his wallet and placed it on the counter below the sugar container so that the owner could see it.

The officer was now relieved of his guilt. He ordered to put the shutter down and proceed.

Three months passed away and they were lucky not to lose anyone from their group in the intense insurgency situation. So they looked forward to receive the next team to replace them.

*Soon they were on their way back and stopped at the same tea shop. This time not only the shop was open the owner was also present. The owner, an old man with meagre resources was very happy to greet fifteen customers.*

*All of them had tea and biscuits. They talked to the old man about his life and the experiences he had while selling tea at such a remote place.*

*The old man had many stories to share, replete with his faith in God. "Oh, Baba, if God is there, why should He keep you in such poverty?" commented one of them.*

*"Do not say like that Sahib! God is actually there. I got a proof three months ago. I was going through very tough times at that time as my only son had been severely beaten by terrorists. I had closed my shop to take him to the hospital. Some medicines were to be purchased but I had no money. No one would give me loan for fear of the terrorists. There was no hope, Sahib".*

*"That day Sahib, I prayed to God for help and Sahib, God walked into my shop that day. When I returned to my shop, I found a Rs 1000 note under the sugar pot. I can't tell you Sahib what that money was worth that day. God exists, Sahib. He does."*

*The faith in his eyes was unflinching. Fifteen pairs of eyes met the eyes of the officer and read the order in his eyes clear and unambiguous. "Keep quiet".*

*The officer got up and paid the bill. He hugged the old man and said, "Yes Baba, I know God does exist. And yes, the tea was wonderful."*

*The fifteen pairs of eyes did not miss to notice the moisture building up in the eyes of their officer, a rare sight.*

We know that God had actually not visited his shop. But we often get an impression through such incidents that He comes to help us exactly whenever we may be in some trouble when we may not be expecting to get any help from anyone.

---

1 Reproduced with the permission of the publisher The Source Publications Pvt. Ltd., Mumbai

# 14

# Human Incarnations of God

Hindus and Christians both believe in incarnations of God.

Christians believe that Christ was an incarnation of God the same way as Hindus believe that Rama and Krishna were also incarnations of God.

As a matter of fact Lord Krishna had on one hand proclaimed Himself to have been an incarnation of God, on the other hand He had also said that God keeps on incarnating Himself in the form of human beings from time to time in the following verse (Verse 7-8 of the fourth chapter) of Bhagvad Gita,

*Yada yada hi dharmasya glanirbhavati bharata*
*Abhythanamadharmasya tadatmanam srijamyaham*
*Paritranaya sadhunang vinashay cha dushkritam*
*Dharmasangsthapanarthay sambhabami yuge yuge*

which translates in English as:

"O Bharata, whenever there is decay of righteousness and there is exaltation of unrighteousness, I Myself come forth for the protection of the good. For the destruction of evil-doers for the sake of firmly establishing righteousness, I am born from age to age."

But what has confused the entire Hindu community is the fact that Rama is believed to have born in Treta-Yuga which commenced on 869000 BCE and went up to 437000 BCE according to the following chart of Hindu Yugas. Who would ever believe it fully well knowing that the man used to live in jungles and caves just like animals only during the Stone Age which had lasted till 3300BCE starting 9300 BCE since Kali-Yuga is believed to have started since 3012 BCE, 5000 years on?

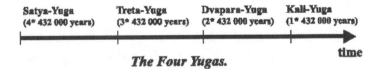

*The Four Yugas.*

Of course we may rely on Saptarishi Timeline of Yugas which specifies that each Yuga may have consisted of only 3000 years.

This Timeline dovetails well to 10th January 5114 BCE, the date of birth calculated by Sunil Sheoran as per Swiss Ephemeris Data (based on NASA JPL data) based on the position of the stars described in Maharshi Valmiki's Ramayana's Bala Kanda, Sarg 18, Shlokas 8/9/10 and the life span of Lord Krishna to have been from 3228 BCE to 3102 BCE as calculated according to Drik Panchang calculations.

The following Timeline would even make everyone happy that Rama had born during Treta-Yuga and Krishna during Dvapar-Yuga only.

Previous Cycle of Time-Line

Satya-Yuga (3000 years) from 10000 BCE to 7000 BCE

Treta-Yuga (3000 years) from 7000 BCE to 4000 BCE

Dvapar-Yuga (3000 years) from 4000 BCE to 1000 BCE

Kali-Yuga (3000 years) from 1000 BCE to 2000 CE

Current Cycle of Time-Line

Kali-Yuga (3000 years) from 2000 CE to 5000 CE

Dvapar-Yuga (3000 years) from 5000 CE to 8000 CE

.... .... ....

Though there are as many as fifty tombolos, the sand bars that rise above the water level and connect the mainland with an island or one island with another island or several islands together, around the world such as the one that connects St Ninian's Isle with the Shetland Mainland and even Ram Setu, the bridge connecting Pamban Island off the south-eastern coast of Tamilnadu and Manna r Island off the north-western coast of Sri Lanka has been listed as one of them the fact that Maharshi Valmiki has mentioned in his Ramayana that it had been constructed by Nal and Neel to let the army of Rama cross over from Indian shore to the Lankan shore around 5076 BCE sets it apart from tombolos. It is very much a man-made bridge because it is of a uniform width all along, it is as wide as 100 meters and is not only as long as 35 km the shoals of the bridge are held together by a white lime-like mortar. So it would be wrong to assume that it should have been only an artefact of nature. In no other country any tombolo has been named to have been constructed as Ram Setu has been named in India.

Though the radiocarbon dating of the shoals used for the bridge verges on around 1,750,000 years, which roughly coincides with the mythical estimate of 'Treta-Yuga' it is quite possible that only the floating shoals used by them may have been that old but the bridge may have been constructed in the year 5076 BCE only.

More so, we have a reason to believe that Nal and Neel should have known how such a bridge should have been constructed as its existence has been validated by NASA by releasing the following image[1] of the bridge taken by a space shuttle on Feb 23, 2003.

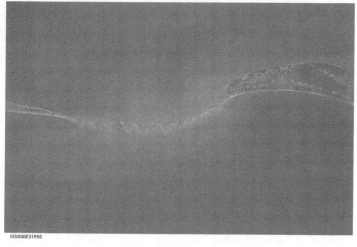

*Image[1] of Ram Setu*

Though some portions of the bridge have now sunk a few meters deep into water it s really amazing that it should have withstood the test of time so well.

Further, even a team of experts had confirmed that the type of the lime stone shoals used to construct it suggests that such stones must have been transported from somewhere else only because they do not match with the local coral reefs.

According to the records of Rameshwaram Temple people had been using the bridge for thousands of years to cross the sea till 1480 when it got damaged at some places by a cyclone.

Though we may not be able to conceptualize the technology Nal and Neel may have used but surely, they must have known the technique of constructing such a bridge over the sea or else how they could have constructed such a bridge?

That they could have joined the shoals so firmly that they are still as firmly held together as they may have been at the time of the construction of the bridge makes us believe that such a bridge could have not been built without a divine hand.

It is of course quite stupefying from where they ought to have brought such a large consignment of the shoals that did not have to sink in water.

Though Maharshi Valmiki had mentioned in his book that this bridge had been constructed by Nal and Neel the mystery surrounding the bridge would have got very much resolved had he also mentioned in his book the place from where they had resourced so many floating stones, millions of them, to construct such a long bridge. However we get a hint that these stones may have been resourced either from the U-shaped structure dating back to 9000 BCE unveiled by National Institute of Oceanography believed to have existed near Nagapattinam which got submerged into the ocean eventually or from the place known as Kumari Kandam surrounding the bridge which fell in the region referred to as Pandya Nadu at that time and had been reigned over by the Pandyan dynasty from around 600 BCE till first half of 17<sup>th</sup> century CE according to Sangam literature but also seems to have got submerged later on, under water.

Whenever there is something that is beyond our comprehension we often ascribe it to a divine hand. But if we believe that there should have been a divine hand behind the construction of this bridge, we indirectly admit that there ought to be some God in the world.

Existence of such a divine power only goes to strengthen our faith in the existence of God. Does the possibility of so long lasting bridge over sea way back in 5076 BCE not stand as a testimony to the existence of God by itself or should we be still hunting for some better proof to substantiate His existence?

---

1 NASA's Photo ID ISS006-E-31850 catalogued at http://eol.jsc.nasa.gov/SearchPhotos

# 15

## Coming in Unison with God

$J$ust think for a while, if we could walk at the speed of light we won't ever come across darkness.

There is something actually more than this to it. If we may walk at the speed of light then only we can come physically in unison with God because He not only walks at the speed of light, He can perhaps walk even faster than light. This incidentally explains why it is difficult for us to come in unison with Him physically. We would never be atheists if we try to understand why it is not possible for us to come physically in unison with Him. We may come in unison with Him only mentally.

Of course God can walk even at our speed to be in unison with us. When He does so, we say He is acting like a human being.

It may not be possible for us to walk at the speed of light but we may anyway imagine ourselves walking at the speed of light in step with Him for a while to understand how it feels to be in unison with Him.

Marilyn Adamson tries to remove the dust of atheism off the plank of our mind through her "Spiritual Adventure Pack" by dispelling some of the misgivings usually harboured by the atheists.

This pack is available at the site EveryStudent.com.

This Pack tells why we should not be atheists.

In her "Spiritual Adventure Pack" Marilyn Adamson tries out to dismiss the arguments put forth by the genre of atheists very effectively to once again establish the validity of the existence of God she has been so strongly scouting since 1996 when Campus Crusade for Christ, International had published her famous article "Is There a God?".

No doubt she has done a fine job. And, why not! After all she was herself an atheist once upon a time. Who can understand the arguments based on which the atheists thrive better than her since she was herself an atheist to begin with. Actually she used to find it quite tough fighting out in arguments her friend who used to not only very firmly believe in the existence God but used to even attribute all the social work she used to do also to God only. She wrote this article actually after researching a lot why her friend so staunchly believed in God.

In this pack she has referred to wars, murders, child abuse, corrupt governments, rapes, greed, complacency toward poverty and hunger, torture, drug addictions fuelled by cartels and sex slavery. The atheists argue why God should at all allow sufferings caused by devastating earthquakes, floods, tsunamis, tornadoes, volcanoes that lack human cause if we think, He is there.

They argue, "Do diseases, cancers, mental disabilities, birth defects and poverty not stand out as evidence against God's existence?" They raise stunning questions like, "Why would you worship a God who allows a child to be raped?"

She says answering such questions is like explaining heart surgery to a rabbit.

She answers the question of suffering through the example why should a mother take her two month old baby to the doctor to get him (or her) immunized allowing him to have a painful prick by pointing out that the infant cannot understand why the mother stands by while this doctor is inflicting pain to him. But mother understands fully well, why.

Doesn't the mother love the child? Mother is by no means some kind of jerk. She loves the child more than anybody else would. Though it would be impossible for the child to comprehend, the mother knows why she gets her child immunized.

Same way, she says, God also knows why He should allow people to have miseries. He is not solely responsible for all such miseries. These accrue to us due to good many reasons for which He alone is not responsible. We too are a party to it. Mostly sufferings are our own creations. The word "own" implies the entire humanity at large not any specific individual alone.

She says, if you begin a relationship with him, you would find out that he is much more deeply, fully involved in caring for you than you could ever have imagined or hoped for.

She refers to the book "Knowing God" of J.I. Packer in which he brings up a good point, the more complex an object, the tougher it is to say you really know it. To know a song, a book, a recipe is fairly easy. Living things become more complicated. If you have a pet dog or cat, you can probably predict how it will likely behave at certain times. You know what it wants and what it is asking you to do.

But knowing a person is even more complicated because people hide some of their thoughts or feelings. Therefore, how well you know someone largely depends on how much they are willing to reveal to you.

What about with God? How well can we possibly know God? It entirely depends upon what God chooses to reveal about him. Doesn't it?

J.I. Packer goes on to say, "We do not make friends with God; God makes friends with us, bringing us to know him by making his love known to us."

That is exactly what she says she experienced and continues to experience.

She quotes from Packer, "All my knowledge of him depends on his sustained initiative in knowing me. He knows me as a friend, one who loves me; and there is no moment when his eye is off me, or his attention distracted from me, and no moment, therefore, when his care falters."

Packer says this, because it is exactly what the Bible says is true of all those who have begun a relationship with God.

And best of all, we don't earn or have to qualify for that relationship.

This is grounded in what God has revealed about himself. From the Bible: "Anyone who does not love does not know God, because God is love. In this the love of God was made manifest among us, that God sent his only Son into the world, so that we might live through him. In this is love, not that we have loved God but that he loved us."

Everything up till now seemed to show that God wants us to have sound reasons we can point to, leading us to believe in him.

Though she did not use to believe earlier what her friend had told her, "A relationship with God and eternal life are free gifts offered to us". But now she says she believes in it.

If we develop a relationship with him, we could be guided by him, and see him work in our lives to become a better person that we could be without him. Just like any significant relationship has an effect on us, knowing God also changes us.

Toward the end, she talks about some disclaimers.

She says we should not have an impression that life would necessarily become easy or you would escape problems, crises, heartaches and pain. You perhaps won't.

Yet you have to decide if you want a relationship with God or not. Do you want him in your life? Do you want him as your God or not?

You have to decide for yourself, whether you want to begin a relationship with him or not.

We stand to gain only, not lose anything if we develop relationship with someone who is way ahead far more intelligent than any of us.

# Profile of the Author

**B**orn in 1939 at Dinga (District Gujrat, West Pakistan), the author is a resident of Lucknow (India). He graduated in Mechanical Engineering from Thapar Engineering College, Patiala in year 1961. He is the Founder Chairman of the Lucknow Chapter of "Computer Society of India" and a Life Fellow of "Indian Institution of Industrial Engineering". His first book "Productivity Management: Concepts & Techniques" was published by Tata-McGraw Hill Publishing Company Limited in year 1991 and another book "The Mathematics of Uncertainties" is under print.

If you may like to contact the author, you may contact him at the following Email ID:
subhashchandrasawhney@gmail.com

Printed in the United States
By Bookmasters